BISCUITS

QUICK & EASY
BISCUITS

70 imaginative recipes
for the busy cook

Valerie Eames

D

Dealerfield

Published 1994 by Salamander Books Ltd.,
129/137 York Way, London N7 9LG.

This edition specially printed for Dealerfield Ltd, 1995

1 3 5 7 9 8 6 4 2

ISBN: 1 85927 068 9

CREDITS

Managing Editor Samantha Gray
Art Director Jane Forster
Photographer Edward Allwright
Home Economist Valerie Eames
Typeset by Bookworm Typesetting, Manchester
Colour Separation by Scantrans Pte. Ltd., Singapore
Jacket Border by Susan Williams (Home Economist)
Edward Allwright (Photographer)
Acorn Studios plc, London
(Computer Graphics)
Printed in Belgium by Proost International Book Production

Contents

Introduction

Cookies, crackers, crumbles, creams and biscuits – all these words conjure up pictures of one irresistible confection.

The word 'biscuit' is derived from the French word meaning 'twice cooked'. This lengthy cooking process dried out biscuits so that they kept well before the days of airtight containers. Today shops offer a vast range of well-flavoured biscuits in eye-catching packets, but few can compete with the flavour, texture and aroma of the freshly baked variety.

Whether you are looking for treats for parties or lunch boxes, beautifully decorated presents or simply something plain and crisp to serve with coffee, you will find all the recipes you need in this book. Some recipes, like those for Florentines and shortbread, macaroons and oatcakes, have been well tested over the years. Traditional favourites have been handed down and many variations added to the list.

If you are new to home-baking, start with the simplest, plainest recipes. The luxurious creams and biscuits for special occasions take a little more time but are well worth the effort. There are fun and colourful biscuits for children both to help make and to eat, and a section on no-bake biscuits, simple to make on the hob.

The special tips help you to get the best results from these recipes and give ideas for variations, decorative finishes and effective storage.

BISCUIT-MAKING EQUIPMENT
The simplest home-made biscuits are easy to prepare with just basic pieces of equipment.
• Use good scales and proper measuring spoons to measure ingredients accurately. Level ingredients in measuring spoons with the back of a knife, and use a jug for large quantities of liquid.
• Have a sieve ready for dry ingredients to remove lumps and incorporate spices and raising agents evenly.

- Use fairly large bowls to allow room for thorough mixing, rubbing in or working by hand.
- An electric mixer will save time and effort when creaming or whisking. Use a metal spoon for folding in.
- A large rolling pin is essential for rolling out evenly. Roll out dough on a cool work top or marble slab, using just the minimum of flour to prevent sticking.
- Use a sharp knife for chopping ingredients, cutting dough cleanly and marking cooked biscuits into portions.
- A palette knife is ideal for transferring unbaked biscuits to baking sheets and baked biscuits to wire racks for cooling.
- Biscuits bake more evenly on flat baking sheets, or baking trays with just low sides. Choose good-quality thick baking sheets as cheap thin ones tend to buckle when hot.
- Cool biscuits on large wire racks so that they do not over-lap and bend out of shape.
- For some recipes you will also need a saucepan and heatproof bowl for melting butter, chocolate etc., a grater, a pastry brush for glazing and non-stick baking paper.

If you plan to bake biscuits regularly it is worth adding the following to your collection of baking equipment:
- A pastry wheel for cutting fancy edges, and a selection of plain and shaped cutters. Metal cutters are preferable as they have a sharper cutting edge than plastic ones.
- Piping equipment − larger bags and nozzles for piping soft doughs and a smaller selection for icings.
- Shortbread moulds and a biscuit press are probably the most expensive items you may want to invest in.

STORING BISCUITS
- Plain un-iced biscuits keep fresh and crisp the longest. Store them in an airtight container in a cool place for up to 2 weeks.
- Richer biscuits, and those

that have been filled or iced will keep for 2-3 days. Biscuits with creamy fillings keep better if stored in an airtight container in the refrigerator.
•Store different types of biscuits separately when possible, particularly those with strong flavours.
•Layer more delicate biscuits with sheets of non-stick paper to protect them.

Freezing biscuits Most rich, firm biscuit doughs with a high proportion of fat freeze well for up to 3 months. Do not freeze doughs containing nuts as the flavour and texture will be spoilt. Either wrap and freeze whole pieces of dough or open-freeze shaped unbaked biscuits. Separate biscuits can be layered with paper, packed in boxes or bags and baked when required from frozen, adding a few minutes to the usual baking time.

Ready-baked biscuits can also be frozen before filling or icing. Pack delicate biscuits carefully, and refresh in a hot oven before serving if wished.

BISCUIT-MAKING METHODS
Rubbed-in method Biscuits made by this method can be plain or enriched with eggs or extra butter. Use chilled butter for rubbing in to prevent the mixture from sticking together. Cut it into small pieces and rub into the flour with your fingertips until the mixture resembles breadcrumbs. Milk or eggs are usually added to bind the dough, which is then shaped or rolled out and cut as required.

Creaming method A wide variety of biscuits are made by creaming, from plain Shrewsbury biscuits to fancy creams.

Allow butter to soften slightly by standing it in a warm place before creaming. Beat together the butter and sugar with a wooden spoon or electric mixer until it is pale, soft and creamy. After adding flour and binding ingredients the dough can be kneaded lightly. If a dough which requires rolling out is too soft, chill it in the refrigerator until firmer. Do not add extra flour or the baked biscuits will be tough.

Melting method Biscuits such as flapjacks, gingerbread and brandy snaps are made by this method. The butter, sugars and syrups are melted together, then the dry ingredients stirred in, often with fruit and nuts. The resulting dough is quite soft because of the high proportion of sugar, but it firms up on cooling. The mixture can then be rolled out, spooned or pressed into tins.

The baked biscuits crisp on cooling, so they either need to be shaped quickly or left to stand for a few minutes before removing from the baking sheets.

Whisked method This method is used for meringue and sponge biscuits, also for thin crisp wafers.

The eggs and sugar are whisked until pale and creamy, preferably with an electric mixer. After melted butter, flour and any flavourings have been added, the soft mixture is ready for spooning or piping on to greased baking sheets.

Refrigerator biscuits These biscuits are usually made by the creaming method, but the dough is too soft to work with until it has been thoroughly chilled. Chilled dough can be kept in the refrigerator for up to a week before slicing and baking.

No-bake biscuits Although these are not true biscuits they are just as delicious and quick to make. The method usually involves melting butter, chocolate and sugar in a saucepan and adding cereals or crushed biscuits, fruit and nuts. The soft mixture can be shaped or pressed into a tin and sets on chilling, resulting in a wonderfully chewy biscuit.

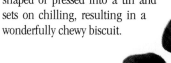

Arrowroot Rings

INGREDIENTS

Makes 48

125 g (4 oz) plain flour

125 g (4 oz) arrowroot

50 g (2 oz) butter

75 g (3 oz) caster sugar

1 egg yolk

4 tbsp milk

1   Preheat the oven to 180°C (350°F/Gas 4). Lighlty grease several baking sheets.

2   Sift the flour and arrowroot into a bowl. Rub in the butter until the mixture resembles fine breadcrumbs. Stir the sugar into the mixture. Add the egg yolk and milk and mix to form a stiff dough. Knead lightly.

3   Roll out on a floured surface to 3 mm (⅛ in) thick. Using a 6 cm (2½ in) fluted cutter, cut out rounds from the dough. Place on the baking sheets and remove the centres with a 2.5 cm (1 in) cutter. Prick with a fork.

4   Knead and re-roll the trimmings. Continue cutting out more rings until all the dough is used up.

5   Bake for 10 minutes or until very lightly browned. Transfer to wire racks to cool.

COOK'S TIPS
If you do not have a cutter small enough to cut out the centres of the rings, use an apple corer or the wide end of an icing nozzle. If cutters stick to the dough, dip them in flour.

Swiss Whirls

1   Preheat the oven to 180°C (350°F/Gas 4). Arrange 20 petits fours cases on baking sheets.

2   Put the butter, icing sugar and vanilla essence in a bowl and beat until light and creamy.

3   Sift the plain flour and cornflour into the mixture and work in well.

4   Spoon the mixture into a piping bag fitted with a medium star nozzle. Pipe whirls into the petits fours cases and decorate each whirl with pieces of angelica and cherry.

5   Bake for 15-18 minutes until very lightly browned. Transfer to a wire rack to cool.

6 When the biscuits are cold, remove the case from each one and dredge with icing sugar.

COOK'S TIP
This mixture can be quite firm to pipe. It will be soft enough if you stand the butter in a warm place before starting and beat the mixture thoroughly.

INGREDIENTS

Makes 20

125 g (4 oz) unsalted butter

25 g (1 oz) icing sugar, sifted

few drops vanilla essence

75 g (3 oz) plain flour

25 g (1 oz) cornflour

small piece of angelica, finely chopped

1 glacé cherry, finely chopped

icing sugar for dredging

Grantham Gingerbreads

INGREDIENTS

Makes 30

125 g (4 oz) butter

350 g (12 oz) caster sugar

1 egg, beaten

250 g (9 oz) self-raising flour

1½ tsp ground ginger

1   Preheat the oven to 150°C (300°F/Gas 2). Lightly grease several baking sheets.

2   Put the butter and sugar in a bowl and beat until light and creamy. Gradually beat in the egg.

3   Sift the flour and ginger into the mixture and work in to make a dough. Knead lightly.

4   Divide the dough into 30 pieces and roll each piece into a ball. Put on the baking sheets, spacing apart.

5   Bake for about 40 minutes until risen, hollow and crisp, and very lightly browned. Cool on wire racks.

Petticoat Tails

1   Put the butter and sugar in a bowl and beat until light and creamy.

2   Sift the flours into the mixture and work in by hand to form a soft dough.

3   Lightly flour the work surface. Divide the dough into 2 pieces and roll out each piece to fit an 18 cm (7 in) sandwich tin.

4   Place the dough in the tins and press in gently. Flute the edges if wished and prick well with a fork. Chill for 30 minutes. Preheat the oven to 150°C(300°F/Gas 2).

5   Bake the shortbread for 40-45 minutes until pale golden.

6   Mark each round into 8 portions and dredge with sugar while hot. Cool in the tins.

COOK'S TIP
For shortbread and other biscuits with a high proportion of fat it is preferable to use butter rather than margarine because of its superior flavour.

INGREDIENTS

Makes 16

225 g (8 oz) butter

75 g (3 oz) caster sugar

250 g (9 oz) plain flour

50 g (2 oz) rice flour

caster sugar to dredge

Langues de Chat

INGREDIENTS

Makes 30

50 g (2 oz) butter

65 g (2½ oz) caster sugar

1 egg, beaten

50 g (2 oz) plain flour

1   Preheat the oven to 220°C (425°F/Gas 7). Lightly grease several baking sheets and line them with non-stick paper.

2   Put the butter and sugar in a bowl and beat until light and creamy. Gradually beat in the egg.

3   Sift the flour into the mixture and fold it in to make a very soft dough.

4   Spoon the mixture into a piping bag fitted with a 6 mm (¼ in) plain nozzle. Pipe 7.5 cm (3 in) lengths on to the baking sheets, spacing them very well apart.

5   Bake for 5 minutes until the edges are lightly browned. Leave to stand for 1 minute before transferring to wire racks to cool.

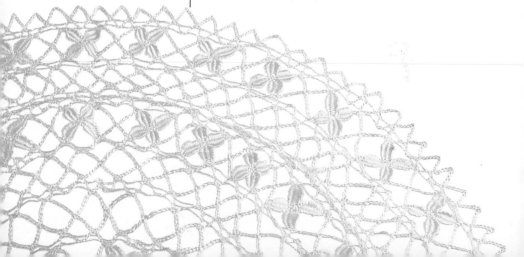

Gingernuts

1 Preheat the oven to 180°C (350°F/Gas 4). Lightly grease 2 baking sheets.

2 Put the butter, syrup, sugar and treacle into a saucepan and stir over a gentle heat until melted. Cool slightly.

3 Sift together the flour, ginger, cinnamon and bicarbonate of soda. Stir into the melted ingredients until smooth.

4 Put 18 rounded teaspoons of the mixture on to the baking sheets, leaving room for spreading. Bake for 10-12 minutes until browned.

5 Leave to stand for 1 minute before transferring to wire racks to cool and harden.

INGREDIENTS

Makes 18

50 g (2 oz) butter

2½ tbsp golden syrup

25 g (1 oz) soft light brown sugar

1½ tbsp black treacle

125 g (4 oz) self-raising flour

1 tsp ground ginger

1 tsp ground cinnamon

½ tsp bicarbonate of soda

Digestive Biscuits

INGREDIENTS

Makes 20

175 g (6 oz) wholemeal
flour

50 g (2 oz) plain flour

75 g (3 oz) butter,
chilled and diced

25 g (1 oz) light soft
brown sugar

1 egg, beaten

1-2 tsp milk

1   Preheat the oven to 200°C (400°F/Gas 6). Lightly grease 2 baking sheets.

2   Mix together the wholemeal and plain flours. Rub in the butter until the mixture resembles fine breadcrumbs.

3   Stir the sugar into the mixture. Add the egg and milk and mix to form a fairly firm dough. Knead lightly. Roll out the dough on a floured surface to a rectangle 30 x 25 cm (12 x 10 in).

4   Using a pastry wheel or knife cut the dough into 6 cm (2½ in) squares. Place on the baking sheets and prick with a fork. Bake for about 12 minutes until lightly browned. Transfer to wire racks and allow to cool.

Wheatgerm Thins

1   Preheat the oven to 190°C (375°F/Gas 5). Lightly grease several baking sheets.

2   Mix together the flours and wheatgerm in a bowl. Rub in the butter until the mixture resembles fine breadcrumbs. Stir in the sugar, add the egg yolk and milk and mix to make a soft dough. Knead gently.

3   Roll out the dough on a floured surface to 3 mm (⅛ in) thick. Cut out rounds with a 6 cm (2½ in) fluted cutter. Place on the baking sheets. Knead and re-roll the trimmings to cut out more rounds until all the dough is used up.

4   Mix together the wheatgerm and sugar to make the topping. Sprinkle over half of each round. Bake for 7-8 minutes until very lightly browned, then transfer to a wire rack to cool. Dredge the second half of each biscuit with icing sugar.

INGREDIENTS

Makes 30

50 g (2 oz) plain wholemeal flour

50 g (2 oz) plain flour, sifted

25 g (1 oz) wheatgerm

50 g (2 oz) butter, chilled and diced

50 g (2 oz) soft light brown sugar

1 egg yolk, beaten

1 tbsp milk

icing sugar to dredge

For the topping

2 tbsp wheatgerm
4 tsp soft light brown sugar

Madeleines

INGREDIENTS

Makes 30

2 eggs, separated

125 g (4 oz) caster sugar

125 g (4 oz) unsalted butter, melted

125 g (4 oz) self-raising flour, sifted

finely grated rind of ½ lemon

icing sugar to dredge

1   Preheat the oven to 190°C (375°F/Gas 5). Lightly grease and flour 30 moulds on madeleine trays.

2   Put the egg yolks and sugar in a bowl and whisk together until pale and creamy. Gradually beat the butter and flour into the mixture.

3   Beat the egg whites lightly with a fork, then beat into the mixture, along with the lemon rind.

4   Three-quarters fill each madeleine mould with mixture and smooth the tops. Bake for 12-15 minutes until lightly browned.

5   Transfer to wire racks to cool, then dredge with icing sugar.

COOK'S TIP
These are traditionally baked in special shell-shaped moulds. If you are unable to find a madeleine tray, use lightly greased tartlet tins.

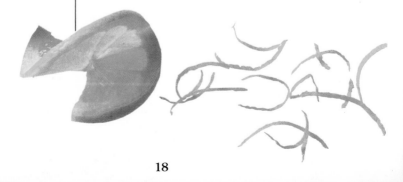

Cinnamon Snaps

1 Preheat the oven to 180°C (350°F/Gas 4). Lightly grease several baking sheets.

2 Put the butter and sugar in a bowl and beat until light and creamy.

3 Sift the flour and cinnamon into the bowl and work into the mixture to make a soft dough. Knead gently.

4 Roll out the dough on a lightly floured surface to about 3 mm (⅛ in) thick.

5 Cut out rounds with a 5 cm (2 in) plain cutter and place on the baking sheets, spacing well apart. Knead and re-roll trimmings to cut out more rounds until all the dough is used up.

6 Dredge the biscuits with caster sugar and bake for 8-9 minutes until just firm to the touch.

7 Leave to stand for a few minutes, then transfer to wire racks and leave to cool.

COOK'S TIP
These biscuits are soft when hot. Leave to cool slightly before removing from the baking sheets to prevent them from bending when handled and cooling mis-shapen.

INGREDIENTS

Makes 30

50 g (2 oz) butter

50 g (2 oz) caster sugar

50 g (2 oz) plain flour

1 tsp ground cinnamon

caster sugar to dredge

Nut and Raisin Oatcakes

INGREDIENTS

Makes 12

75 g (3 oz) plain flour

1 tsp baking powder

50 g (2 oz) butter,
chilled and diced

75 g (3 oz) medium
oatmeal

75 g (3 oz) mixed nuts
and raisins, chopped

2 tbsp milk

1　Preheat the oven to 180°C (350°F/Gas 4). Lightly grease 2 baking sheets.

2　Sift the flour and baking powder into a bowl. Rub in the butter until the mixture resembles fine breadcrumbs.

3　Stir the oatmeal and nuts and raisins into the mixture. Add the milk and mix to make a firm dough. Knead gently.

4　Roll out the dough on a floured surface to 6 mm (¼ in) thick. Cut out rounds with a 5.5 cm (2¼ in) fluted cutter. Place on the baking sheets. Knead and re-roll the trimmings. Continue cutting out more rounds until all the dough is used up.

5　Bake for about 12 minutes until very lightly browned. Transfer to a wire rack to cool.

COOK'S TIP
Buy a pack of ready-mixed nuts and raisins, including almonds, hazelnuts and peanuts.

Lemon and Lime Thins

1   Preheat the oven to 180°C (350°F/Gas 4). Lightly grease several baking sheets.

2   Finely grate the rind from the lemons and limes. Reserve a little to decorate the biscuits.

3   Put the butter, sugar and grated rind in a bowl and beat until light and creamy. Beat in the egg yolk.

4   Sift the flour into the bowl and mix in to make a smooth dough. Knead lightly.

5   Roll out the dough on a floured surface to 3 mm (⅛ in) thick.

6   Cut out rounds with a 5 cm (2 in) cutter and place on the baking sheets. Knead and re-roll trimmings to cut out more rounds until all the dough is used up.

7   Bake for 8-9 minutes until very lightly browned, then transfer to wire racks to cool.

8   Sprinkle the biscuits with reserved lemon and lime rinds and dredge with icing sugar.

COOK'S TIP
For a perfect finish use a tea strainer to dredge the biscuits evenly and lightly with icing sugar.

INGREDIENTS

Makes 60

2 lemons

2 limes

125 g (4 oz) butter

75 g (3 oz) caster sugar

1 egg yolk, beaten

150 g (5 oz) self-raising flour

icing sugar to dredge

Fruity Flapjacks

INGREDIENTS

Makes 16

125 g (4 oz) butter

100 g (3½ oz) soft light
brown sugar

50 g (2 oz) golden syrup

225 g (8 oz) rolled oats

65 g (2½ oz) currants

65 g (2½ oz) stoned
dates, chopped

50 g (2 oz) glacé
cherries, chopped

1   Preheat the oven to 190°C (375°F/Gas 5). Lightly grease a 28 x 18 cm (11 x 7 in) Swiss roll tin.

2   Put the butter, sugar and syrup into a saucepan and stir over a gentle heat until melted.

3   Stir in the oats, currants, dates and cherries. Spoon the mixture into the tin, pressing down well. Bake for 20-25 minutes until lightly browned.

4   Leave to cool for 5 minutes, then mark into 16 fingers, cutting into 4 lengthwise and 4 widthwise. Cool in the tin.

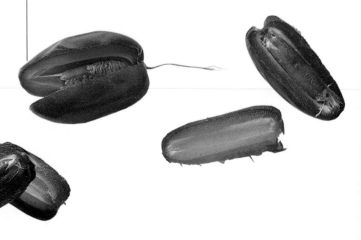

Sesame and Sunflower Bars

1   Preheat the oven to 180°C (350°F/Gas 4). Lightly grease an 18 cm (7 in) square tin and line it with non-stick paper.

2   Put the butter, sugar and syrup into a saucepan and stir over a gentle heat until melted. Stir in the oats and seeds.

3   Spoon the mixture into the tin, pressing down well. Bake for about 30 minutes or until browned and firm to touch.

4   Leave to cool for a few minutes, then mark into bars. Divide the square in half and cut each into 7 pieces. Cool in the tin.

VARIATION
Replace the sunflower seeds with pumpkin seeds and a few chopped nuts.

INGREDIENTS

Makes 14

125 g (4 oz) butter

75 g (3 oz) light muscovado sugar

75 g (3 oz) golden syrup

160 g (5½ oz) rolled oats

2 tbsp sunflower seeds

25 g (1 oz) sesame seeds

Orange Shrewsbury Biscuits

INGREDIENTS

Makes 30

125 g (4 oz) butter

150 g (5 oz) caster sugar

1 egg yolk, beaten

grated rind of ½ orange

225 g (8 oz) plain flour

2 tbsp orange juice

65 g (2½ oz) icing sugar, sifted

1 tbsp orange juice

grated rind of ½ orange

1　Lightly grease several sheets. Put the butter and sugar in a bowl and beat until light and creamy. Beat in the egg yolk and orange rind.

2　Sift the flour into the bowl and stir in the orange juice. Mix to make a fairly firm dough.

3　Knead the dough lightly. Roll out on a lightly floured surface to about 5 mm (¼ in) thick.

4　Cut out rounds with a 6 cm (2½ in) fluted cutter and place on the baking sheets. Knead and re-roll trimmings to cut out more rounds until all the dough is used up. Chill for 30 minutes. Preheat the oven to 180°C (350°F/Gas 4).

5　Bake the biscuits for 15-20 minutes until lightly browned. Transfer to wire racks to cool.

6　Meanwhile, make the icing. Beat together the icing sugar, orange juice and orange rind.

7　Drizzle or spread the icing over the biscuits and leave to set.

Almond Macaroons

1   Preheat the oven to 180°C (350°F/Gas 4). Line 2 or 3 baking sheets with rice paper.

2   Put the egg whites in a clean, grease-free bowl. Whisk until stiff but not dry. Gently fold in the sugar, ground almonds and almond essence.

3   Spoon the mixture into a piping bag fitted with a 1 cm (½ in) plain nozzle. Pipe small rounds on to the baking sheets, spacing well apart. Top with halved almonds.

4   Bake for 20 minutes until lightly browned. Leave to cool on the baking sheets.

5   Remove the cold macaroons, tearing away excess rice paper.

INGREDIENTS

Makes 28

rice paper

2 egg whites

175 g (6 oz) caster sugar

175 g (6 oz) ground almonds

few drops almond essence

14 blanched almonds, halved

Pecan and Raisin Cookies

INGREDIENTS

Makes 24

150 g (5 oz) butter

75 g (3 oz) light muscovado sugar

50 g (2 oz) caster sugar

1 egg, beaten

few drops vanilla essence

175 g (6 oz) plain flour

½ tsp bicarbonate of soda

100 g (3½ oz) pecan nuts, chopped

50 g (2 oz) raisins

1   Preheat the oven to 180°C (350°F/Gas 4). Lightly grease several baking sheets.

2   Put the butter and sugars in a bowl and beat until light and creamy. Beat in the egg and vanilla essence.

3   Sift the flour and bicarbonate of soda into the bowl. Stir in thoroughly along with the pecan nuts and raisins.

4   Put 24 heaped teaspoonfuls of the mixture on to the baking sheets, spacing well apart.

5   Bake for 15 minutes until lightly browned. Leave to stand for 1 minute before transferring to a wire rack to cool.

Chocolate Coconut Macaroons

1 Preheat the oven to 160°C (325°F/Gas 3). Line 2 or 3 baking sheets with non-stick paper.

2 Put the whole egg and the egg white in a bowl and whisk until soft and light.

3 Gradually whisk in the caster sugar, then whisk in the cocoa and fold in the coconut.

4 Place 24 heaped teaspoonfuls of the mixture on to the baking sheets, spacing them well apart. Top with chocolate chips, if liked.

5 Bake for 20 minutes or until just firm to the touch. Leave to stand for a few minutes before transferring to a wire rack to cool.

INGREDIENTS

Makes 24

1 egg

1 egg white

125 g (4 oz) caster sugar

25 g (1 oz) cocoa, sifted

225 g (8 oz) desiccated coconut

chocolate chips to top (optional)

Peanut Butter Cookies

INGREDIENTS

Makes 20

75 g (3 oz) butter

75 g (3 oz) crunchy
peanut butter

65 g (2½ oz) light
muscovado sugar

50 g (2 oz) caster sugar

1 egg, beaten

150 g (5 oz) self-raising
flour

1   Preheat the oven to 180°C (350°F/Gas 4). Lightly grease 2 or 3 baking sheets.

2   Put the butter, peanut butter and sugars into a bowl and beat until soft and creamy. Beat in the egg.

3   Sift the flour into the bowl and stir in thoroughly. Put 20 heaped teaspoonfuls of the mixture onto the baking sheets, spacing them well apart.

4   Bake for 15-20 minutes until slightly risen and browned. Transfer to a wire rack to cool.

Apricot Squares

1 Lightly grease 2 or 3 baking sheets. Sift the flour into a bowl. Rub in the butter until the mixture resembles coarse breadcrumbs.

2 Sift in the icing sugar. Stir in the egg yolk, milk and vanilla essence and mix well to form a soft dough. Knead lightly.

3 Divide the dough into 2 pieces and roll out each piece on a lightly floured surface to a rectangle 28 x 23 cm (11 x 9 in).

4 Arrange the apricots over one piece of dough and lay the second piece on top. Press down gently with rolling pin to make rectangle larger.

5 Cut into pieces about 5 cm (2 in) square and place on the baking sheets.

6 Lightly score the biscuits with a knife and chill for 30 minutes. Preheat the oven to 200°C (400°F/Gas 6).

7 Bake the squares for 15 minutes or until very lightly browned. Transfer to wire racks to cool. Dredge with icing sugar.

INGREDIENTS

Makes 30

225 g (8 oz) plain flour

125 g (4 oz) butter, chilled and diced

75 g (3 oz) icing sugar

1 egg yolk, beaten

2 tbsp milk

few drops vanilla essence

175 g (6 oz) ready-to-eat dried apricots, very finely chopped

icing sugar for dredging

Peanut and Syrup Biscuits

INGREDIENTS

Makes 20

75 g (3 oz) butter

50 g (2 oz) light muscovado sugar

1 egg yolk, beaten

125 g (4 oz) self-raising flour

For the topping

1½ tsp golden syrup

25 g (1 oz) skinned peanuts, chopped

1   Preheat the oven to 190°C (375°F/Gas 5). Lightly grease 2 or 3 baking sheets.

2   Put the butter and sugar in a bowl and beat until light and creamy. Beat in the egg yolk.

3   Sift the flour into the bowl and mix in to make a smooth dough. Knead gently.

4   Roll out the dough on a floured surface to 3 mm (⅛ in) thick. Cut out 5 cm (2 in) shapes and place on the baking sheets. Knead and re-roll the trimmings to cut out more shapes until all the dough is used up.

5   Warm the syrup and drizzle it in the centre of the biscuits. Sprinkle with the chopped peanuts.

6   Bake for about 8 minutes until golden brown. Transfer to a wire rack to cool.

COOK'S TIP
These biscuits are best eaten within 2 or 3 days as they lose their crispness.

Sultana Wedges

1   Preheat the oven to 190°C (375°F/Gas 5). Lightly grease 2 or 3 baking sheets.

2   Put the butter and sugar in a bowl and beat until light and creamy. Beat in the egg yolk.

3   Sift together the flour, spice and bicarbonate of soda. Add to the mixture with the soured cream and sultanas. Mix thoroughly to form a soft dough.

4   Divide the dough into 4 pieces. Roll each piece out on a lightly floured surface to form a 15 cm (6 in) round.

5   Cut each round into 6 wedges and place on baking sheets.

6   Bake for 16-18 minutes until lightly browned. Transfer to a wire rack to cool.

COOK'S TIP
Several biscuit recipes call for soft light brown and light muscovado sugar. Either can be used, but muscovado sugar adds a more distinctive flavour and colour.

INGREDIENTS

Makes 24

125 g (4 oz) butter

150 g (5 oz) light muscovado sugar

1 egg yolk, beaten

225 g (8 oz) self-raising flour

½ tsp mixed spice

¼ tsp bicarbonate of soda

125 ml (4 fl oz) soured cream

75 g (3 oz) sultanas

Anzac Biscuits

INGREDIENTS

Makes 20

65 g (2½ oz) butter

1 tbsp golden syrup

¼ tsp bicarbonate of soda

75 g (3 oz) caster sugar

50 g (2 oz) plain flour, sifted

50 g (2 oz) rolled oats

50 g (2 oz) desiccated coconut

1   Preheat the oven to 150°C (300°F/Gas 2). Lightly grease 2 or 3 baking sheets.

2   Put the butter and syrup into a saucepan and stir over a gentle heat until melted.

3   Dissolve the bicarbonate of soda in 1 tbsp of water. Stir into the melted mixture. Add the sugar, flour, oats and coconut to the saucepan and mix thoroughly.

4   Put teaspoonfuls of the mixture on to the baking sheets, spacing them well apart. Bake for 20 minutes until golden. Transfer to a wire rack to cool.

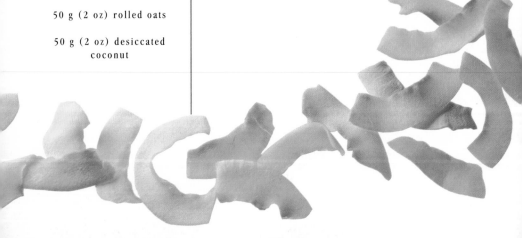

Hazelnut and Honey Bows

1   Put the butter and honey in a bowl and beat until light and creamy. Sift in the flour, then add the ground hazelnuts and work together to form a soft dough.

2   Knead lightly on a floured surface and shape into a roll about 15 cm (6 in) long. Wrap the dough in greaseproof paper and chill for 3-4 hours.

3   When required, preheat the oven to 180°C (350°F/Gas 4). Lightly grease several baking sheets.

4   Cut the chilled dough into 4 mm (⅙ in) thick slices. Cut each slice in half and press the rounded ends together to form a bow.

5   Place the bows on the baking sheets and press a hazelnut in the centre of each one.

6   Bake for 8 minutes until lightly browned. Leave to stand for 1 minute before transferring to a wire rack to cool.

COOK'S TIP
Roasted, chopped hazelnuts can be bought ready prepared to save time.

INGREDIENTS

Makes 36

75 g (3 oz) butter

75 g (3 oz) set honey

150 g (5 oz) plain flour

75 g (3 oz) roasted ground hazelnuts

36 whole blanched hazelnuts

Mint Chocolate Crumbles

INGREDIENTS

Makes 40

150 g (5 oz) butter

75 g (3 oz) icing sugar, sifted

1 egg yolk, beaten

75 g (3 oz) plain chocolate

2 tbsp milk

200 g (7 oz) self-raising flour

125 g (4 oz) mint chocolate sticks

1   Put the butter and sugar in a bowl and beat until light and creamy. Beat in the egg yolk.

2   Break up the chocolate and put in a small saucepan with the milk. Stir over a very gentle heat until melted.

3   Sift the flour into the butter mixture, then add the chocolate milk and work together to form a very soft dough.

4   Lightly flour a large piece of greaseproof paper. Turn out the dough onto the paper and, using a knife, shape into a roll about 25 cm (10 in) long. Wrap up the roll and chill for 4-5 hours.

5   When required preheat the oven to 190°C (375°F/Gas 5). Lightly grease several baking sheets.

6   Cut the chilled dough into 5 mm (¼ in) thick slices. Place on the baking sheets.

7   Bake for 10-12 minutes until just firm to the touch. Leave to stand for a few minutes, then transfer to wire racks to cool.

8   To decorate, melt the mint chocolate sticks in a bowl over a pan of hot water. Drizzle over the biscuits and leave to set.

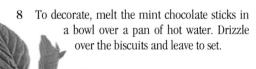

Coffee Jumbles

1   Put the butter and sugar in a bowl and beat until light and creamy. Beat in the egg yolk.

2   Dissolve the coffee granules in 2 tsp of warm water.

3   Sift the flour into the creamed mixture and mix in with the coffee to make a soft dough.

4   Knead the dough on a lightly floured surface to blend in the coffee thoroughly. Wrap the dough in greaseproof paper and chill for at least 30 minutes. Lightly grease 2 or 3 baking sheets.

5   When required, cut off small pieces of dough and roll in caster sugar into thin strips 15 cm (6 in) long. Twist into 'S' shapes and place on the baking sheets. Chill for 30 minutes. Preheat the oven to 180°C (350°F/Gas 4).

6   Bake for 12-15 minutes until just firm to the touch. Transfer to a wire rack to cool.

INGREDIENTS

Makes 26

125 g (4 oz) butter

125 g (4 oz) caster sugar

1 egg yolk, beaten

1 tbsp instant coffee granules

225 g (8 oz) plain flour

a little extra caster sugar for rolling

Choc Cherry Slices

INGREDIENTS

Makes 40

150 g (5 oz) butter

150 g (5 oz) caster sugar

1 egg yolk, beaten

200 g (7 oz) plain flour

25 g (1 oz) cocoa

1 tbsp milk

125 g (4 oz) glacé
cherries

1   Put the butter and sugar in a bowl and beat until light and creamy. Beat in the egg yolk.

2   Sift the flour and cocoa into a bowl, then add the milk and work together to form a soft dough.

3   Turn out the dough on to a lightly floured surface and knead gently, incorporating the glacé cherries. Shape into a roll about 25 cm (10 in) long. Wrap in greaseproof paper and chill for 3-4 hours.

4   When required, preheat the oven to 190°C (375°F/Gas 5). Lightly grease several baking sheets.

5   Cut the chilled dough into 6 mm (¼ in) thick slices. Place on the baking sheets. Bake for 8 minutes until just firm to the touch, then transfer to a wire rack to cool.

COOK'S TIP
Wrapped refrigerator biscuit doughs can be kept chilled for up to a week. Slice off or shape and bake biscuits as you need them.

Marbled Butter Biscuits

1   Prepare each dough separately. For each put the butter and sugar in a bowl and beat until light and creamy. Then sift in the flour, adding the milk or egg yolk and work together.

2   Turn out each dough onto a lightly floured surface and knead gently. Flatten out slightly, then lay one piece on top of the other, and fold together to give a marbled effect.

3   Shape the dough into a roll about 25 cm (10 in) long. Wrap in greaseproof paper and chill for 3-4 hours.

4   When required, preheat the oven to 190°C (375°F/Gas 5). Lightly grease several baking sheets.

5   Cut the chilled dough into 6 mm (¼ in) thick slices. Place on the baking sheets.

6   Bake for 8 minutes or until very lightly browned. Transfer carefully to wire racks to cool.

INGREDIENTS

Makes 40

For the light dough

65 g (2½ oz) butter

65 g (2½ oz) caster sugar

125 g (4 oz) self-raising flour

2 tsp milk or one egg yolk

For the dark dough

65 g (2½ oz) butter

65 g (2½ oz) soft dark brown sugar

125 g (4 oz) self-raising flour

1 egg yolk, beaten

Orange and Lemon Buttons

INGREDIENTS

Makes 32

125 g (4 oz) butter

75 g (3 oz) caster sugar

100 g (3½ oz) self-raising flour

50 g (2 oz) rolled oats, plus 2 tbsp for coating

75 g (3 oz) icing sugar

1 tsp orange juice

1 tsp lemon juice

few drops of orange and yellow food colouring

small orange and yellow sweets

1   Preheat the oven to 190°C (375°F/Gas 5). Lightly grease 2 or 3 baking sheets.

2   Put the butter and sugar in a bowl and beat until light and creamy. Sift the flour into the bowl, then add the oats and mix well to form a fairly soft dough.

3   Using lightly floured hands, roll the dough into small balls, each about the size of an unshelled hazelnut. Roll in the extra oats and place on the baking sheets.

4   Bake for 10 minutes or until golden. Transfer to wire racks to cool.

5   To decorate, divide the icing sugar between 2 bowls. Stir the orange juice and orange colouring into one bowl, and lemon juice and yellow colouring into the other.

6   Spoon a little icing on to each button and top each with a sweet. Leave to set.

Malted Milk Shapes

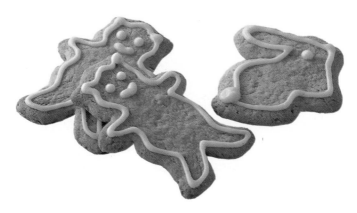

1 Preheat the oven to 190°C (375°F/Gas 5) and lightly grease 2 baking sheets.

2 Put the butter and sugar in a bowl and beat until light and creamy. Gradually beat in the egg and syrup.

3 Sift the flour into the mixture. Add the malted drink powder and rolled oats and mix well to make a soft dough. Knead lightly.

4 Roll out on a floured surface to 4 mm (⅙ in) thick. Cut out animals with 7.5 cm (3 in) cutters and place on the baking sheets. Knead and re-roll the trimmings to cut out more animals until all the dough is used up.

5 Bake for 7-8 minutes until browned. Transfer to wire racks.

6 Meanwhile, make the icing. Blend the icing sugar with water until smooth and thick. Colour with a few drops of food colouring if wished. Use to decorate the biscuits, then leave them to dry.

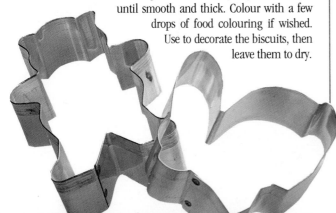

INGREDIENTS

Makes 30

75 g (3 oz) butter

100 g (3½ oz) caster sugar

1 egg, beaten

2 tbsp golden syrup

200 g (7 oz) self-raising flour

50 g (2 oz) malted drink powder

50 g (2 oz) rolled oats

For the icing

50 g (2 oz) icing sugar, sifted

about 1½ tsp warm water

food colouring

Neapolitan Slices

INGREDIENTS

Makes 24

75 g (3 oz) butter

50 g (2 oz) caster sugar

125 g (4 oz) plain flour,
plus 2 tbsp

few drops vanilla essence

few drops pink food
colouring

1 tbsp drinking chocolate

a little beaten egg white

1   Put the butter and sugar in a bowl and beat until light and creamy. Sift over 125 g (4 oz) flour and work in to form a soft dough. Turn out the dough on to a floured surface and divide into 3 equal pieces.

2   Knead the vanilla essence and 1 tbsp flour into one piece. Knead the colouring and 1 tbsp flour into the second piece. Knead the drinking chocolate into the third piece.

3   Roll out each piece of dough into a rectangle measuring 10 x 7.5 cm (4 x 3 in). Place the rectangles on top of each other, brushing between the layers with egg white.

4   Wrap the dough in greaseproof paper and chill for at least 30 minutes. Preheat the oven to 180°C (350°F/Gas 4) and grease 2 baking sheets.

5   Cut the dough into 8 mm (⅓ in) thick slices and cut each slice in half. Place on the baking sheets.

6   Bake for 15-18 minutes until lightly browned. Transfer to wire racks to cool.

Raspberry and Coconut Splits

1   Preheat the oven to 180°C (350°F/Gas 4). Lightly grease 2 baking sheets.

2   Put the butter and sugar in a bowl and beat until light and creamy. Beat in the egg yolk.

3   Sift the flour into the bowl, add the coconut and mix together to make a firm dough. Knead lightly on a floured surface and divide into two equal pieces.

4   Shape each piece into a 20 cm (8 in) roll. Place on the baking sheets. Using a knife handle, make an indentation down the centre of each roll. Fill with the jam. Sprinkle the splits with coconut.

5   Bake for 20 minutes until golden brown. Stand for a few minutes before cutting into 12 splits. Transfer to a wire rack to cool.

INGREDIENTS

Makes 12

50 g (2 oz) butter

50 g (2 oz) caster sugar

1 egg yolk, beaten

125 g (4 oz) self-raising flour

25 g (1 oz) desiccated coconut

2 tbsp raspberry jam

a little extra desiccated coconut

Cornflake Munchies

INGREDIENTS

Makes 24

175 g (6 oz) butter

125 g (4 oz) soft light
brown sugar

1 egg, beaten

175 g (6 oz) self-raising
flour

3 tbsp cocoa

50 g (2 oz) cornflakes,
lightly crushed

75 g (3 oz) raisins

1   Preheat the oven to 180°C (350°F/Gas 4). Lightly grease 2 or 3 baking sheets.

2   Put the butter and sugar in a bowl and beat until light and creamy. Gradually beat in the egg.

3   Sift the flour and cocoa into the bowl, add the cornflakes and raisins and mix together thoroughly. Place 24 heaped teaspoonfuls of the mixture onto the baking sheets.

4   Bake for 15-18 minutes until just firm to the touch. Transfer to a wire rack to cool.

Hoops and Sticks

1   Preheat the oven to 180°C (350°F/Gas 4). Lightly grease 2 baking sheets.

2   Put the butter and sugar in a bowl and beat until light and creamy. Beat in the egg yolk. Sift flour into the bowl and mix in.

3   Divide the mixture into 2 pieces and add cocoa to one.

4   Add a little milk to each mixture and mix in to make smooth doughs. Knead gently.

5   Divide the plain and chocolate doughs into 10 pieces each. Roll each piece on a floured surface into a thick strand 18 cm (7 in) long.

6   Twist the plain and chocolate strands together and form 5 twists into hoops. Place the hoops and sticks on the baking sheets and chill for 30 minutes.

7   Bake for 12-15 minutes until very lightly browned. Transfer to a wire rack to cool.

INGREDIENTS

Makes 10

50 g (2 oz) butter

50 g (2 oz) caster sugar

1 egg yolk, beaten

150 g (5 oz) plain flour

2 tsp cocoa, sifted

1½ tbsp milk

Jumbo Choc-Chip Cookies

INGREDIENTS

Makes 8

125 g (4 oz) butter

75 g (3 oz) soft light brown sugar

50 g (2 oz) caster sugar

1 egg, beaten

175 g (6 oz) self-raising flour

50 g (2 oz) milk chocolate buttons

50 g (2 oz) white chocolate buttons

1   Preheat the oven to 180°C (350°F/Gas 4). Lightly grease several baking sheets.

2   Put the butter and sugars in a bowl and beat until light and creamy. Gradually beat in the egg.

3   Sift the flour into the bowl and stir into the mixture with the milk and white chocolate buttons.

4   Place 8 heaped dessertspoons of the mixture on to baking sheets, spacing them very well apart. Shape into rounds and flatten slightly.

5   Bake the cookies for 20-25 minutes until browned. Leave to stand for a few minutes before transferring to a wire rack to cool.

COOK'S TIP
Allow plenty of space on the baking sheet between these cookies as they spread a lot while baking.

Gingerbread Snakes

1   Preheat the oven to 160°C (325°F/Gas 3). Lightly grease 2 or 3 baking sheets.

2   Put the sugar, butter and syrup into a saucepan. Stir over a gentle heat until melted. Cool slightly.

3   Sift together the flour, ginger and bicarbonate of soda. Mix into the melted ingredients with the egg to form a smooth dough.

4   Turn out the dough on to a floured surface and knead lightly. Roll out to about 5 mm (¼ in) thick. Using a sharp knife, cut out snake shapes 12.5-15 cm (5-6 in) long. Place on baking sheets and score markings on the snakes.

5   Knead and re-roll trimmings. Cut out more snakes.

6   Bake for 15 minutes until just firm to the touch. Stand for a few minutes before transferring to a wire rack to cool.

7   To decorate, blend the icing sugar with about 4 tsp warm water, adding food colouring if wished. Pipe icing on to the snakes and top with dragées and sweets. Leave to set.

COOK'S TIP
This dough is also ideal for making gingerbread people, animals or fancy shapes.

INGREDIENTS

Makes 10-12

75 g (3 oz) soft light brown sugar

50 g (2 oz) butter

3 tbsp golden syrup

225 g (8 oz) plain flour

1 tsp ground ginger

¼ tsp bicarbonate of soda

½ beaten egg

150 g (5 oz) icing sugar, sifted, food colouring, coloured dragées, small sweets

Golden Honey Treats

INGREDIENTS

Makes 30

125 g (4 oz) butter

125 g (4 oz) set honey

1 egg yolk, beaten

225 g (8 oz) plain flour

milk to glaze

For the icing

25 g (1 oz) milk chocolate

1 tbsp set honey

1 tbsp icing sugar, sifted

1 Preheat the oven to 190°C (375°F/Gas 5). Lightly grease 2 or 3 baking sheets.

2 Put the butter and honey in a bowl and beat until light and creamy. Beat in the egg yolk.

3 Sift the flour into the mixture and work in well to make a smooth dough. Knead gently.

4 Divide the dough into 30 pieces and roll each piece into a ball. Place on the baking sheets. Mark each ball with a knife and brush with milk.

5 Bake for 10-12 minutes until golden brown. Transfer to wire racks to cool.

6 To make the icing, melt together the chocolate and honey in a small bowl placed over a pan of hot water. Beat in the icing sugar and leave until thick enough to pipe.

7 Spoon the icing into a piping bag fitted with a fine nozzle. Pipe lines on to the biscuits and leave to set.

Honey and Ginger Rings

1 Preheat the oven to 180°C (350°F/Gas 4). Lightly grease several baking sheets.

2 Put the sugar and butter in a bowl and beat until light and creamy.

3 Sift together the flour, ginger and bicarbonate of soda. Add to the creamed mixture and mix in with the milk to make a smooth dough. Knead lightly.

4 Roll out the dough on a floured surface to 3 mm (⅛ in) thick. Cut out rounds with a 5 cm (2 in) cutter. Place on the baking sheets and remove the centres with a 2 cm (¾ in) cutter.

5 Knead and re-roll the trimmings to cut out more rings until all the dough is used up.

6 Bake for 7-8 minutes until lightly browned, then transfer to wire racks to cool.

7 Meanwhile, make the filling. Put the butter, honey, sifted icing sugar and ginger in a bowl and beat until light and creamy.

8 Sandwich the rings together with the filling and keep in a cool place.

INGREDIENTS

Makes about 44

150 g (5 oz) soft light brown sugar

125 g (4 oz) butter

225 g (8 oz) self-raising flour

2 tsp ground ginger

1½ tsp bicarbonate of soda

2 tbsp milk

For the filling

75 g (3 oz) butter

75 g (3 oz) set honey

75 g (3 oz) icing sugar

40 g (1½ oz) stem ginger, finely chopped

Cardamom and Lemon Wafers

INGREDIENTS

Makes 18

50 g (2 oz) butter

65 g (2½ oz) caster sugar

1 egg, beaten

50 g (2 oz) plain flour

1¼ tsp ground cardamom

icing sugar to dredge

For the filling

125 g (4 oz) icing sugar,
sifted

40 g (1½ oz) butter

juice and finely grated
rind of ¼ lemon

1   Preheat the oven to 190°C (375°F/Gas 5). Line several baking sheets with non-stick paper.

2   Put the butter and sugar in a bowl and beat until light and creamy. Gradually beat in the egg. Sift together the flour and cardamom and fold into the mixture.

3   Drop 36 small teaspoons of the mixture on to the baking sheets and spread into 5 cm (2 in) rounds.

4   Bake for 5-7 minutes until edges are lightly browned. Leave to stand for 1 minute before transferring to wire racks to cool.

5   Meanwhile, make the filling. Put the icing sugar, butter, lemon juice and rind in a bowl. Beat until light and creamy.

6   Sandwich the cooled biscuits together, dredge with icing sugar and keep in a cool place.

Dark Chocolate Delights

1   Preheat the oven to 180°C (350°F/Gas 4). Lightly grease several baking sheets.

2   Put the butter and sifted sugar in a bowl and beat until light and creamy. Gradually beat in the egg.

3   Sift together the flour, cocoa and baking powder. Add to mixture and work in to make a smooth dough. Knead lightly.

4   Roll out on a floured surface to 3 mm (⅛ in) thick. Cut out strips 3 cm (1¼ in) wide, then cut each strip diagonally to make diamond shapes. Place on the baking sheets. Knead and re-roll trimmings to cut out more diamonds until all the dough is used up.

5   Bake for 7-8 minutes until just firm to touch then transfer to wire racks to cool.

6   Meanwhile, make the filling. Melt the chocolate in a bowl placed over a pan of hot water. Remove from the heat, add the sifted sugar, butter and milk, then beat until light and creamy. Sandwich the diamonds together.

7   To finish, melt the remaining chocolate and dip in the top of each biscuit to coat. Leave in a cool place to set.

INGREDIENTS

Makes 40

125 g (4 oz) butter

75 g (3 oz) icing sugar

1 egg, beaten

200 g (7 oz) plain flour

25 g (1 oz) cocoa

½ tsp baking powder

175 g (6 oz) plain
chocolate to finish

For the filling

40 g (1½ oz) plain
chocolate

75 g (3 oz) icing sugar

40 g (1½ oz) butter

2 tsp milk

Yoghurt Crunch Creams

INGREDIENTS

Makes 20

75 g (3 oz) butter

75 g (3 oz) soft light brown sugar

1 egg yolk, beaten

140 g (4½ oz) self-raising flour

40 g (1½ oz) chopped roasted hazelnuts

25 g (1 oz) rolled oats

For the filling

175 g (6 oz) icing sugar, sifted

75 g (3 oz) butter

3 tbsp Greek yoghurt

1   Preheat the oven to 180°C (350°F/Gas 4). Lightly grease several baking sheets.

2   Put the butter and sugar in a bowl and beat until light and creamy. Beat in the egg yolk.

3   Sift the flour into a bowl, add the nuts and oats and mix into the creamed mixture to make a firm dough. Knead lightly.

4   Roll out the dough on a floured surface 4 mm (⅙ in) thick. Cut out rounds with a 5 cm (2 in) cutter. Place on the baking sheets and remove the centres from half the rounds with a 2 cm (¾ in) cutter. Knead and re-roll trimmings to cut out more rounds and rings until all the dough is used up.

5   Bake for 6-7 minutes until lightly browned, then transfer to wire racks to cool.

6   Meanwhile make the filling. Put the sugar, butter and yoghurt in a bowl and beat until light and creamy.

7   Spread the filling on the biscuit rounds and top with rings. Keep in a cool place.

Fudgy Mocha Fingers

1   Preheat the oven to 180°C (350°F/Gas 4). Lightly grease several baking sheets.

2   Dissolve the coffee granules in the water. Put the butter and sugar in a bowl and beat, then beat in the egg yolk and coffee.

3   Sift together the flour and cornflour. Add to the creamed mixture and mix in thoroughly to make a smooth dough.

4   Knead the dough lightly to ensure the coffee blends in. Roll out on a floured surface to 3 mm (⅛ in) thick. Cut out fingers about 5.5 x 2.5 cm (2¼ x 1 in) in size and place on the baking sheets. Knead and re-roll the trimmings to cut out more fingers.

5   Bake for 6-7 minutes until lightly browned then transfer to wire racks to cool.

6   Meanwhile make the filling. Put the coffee and water in a bowl placed over a pan of hot water. Stir to dissolve. Break up the fudge fingers and add to the bowl. Stir occasionally until just soft.

7   Remove the bowl from the heat and whisk in the cream until the filling is smooth and slightly thick. Chill until firm enough to sandwich the biscuits. Dredge with icing sugar.

INGREDIENTS

Makes 42

1 tbsp instant coffee
granules

1 tbsp warm water

75 g (3 oz) butter

75 g (3 oz) caster sugar

1 egg yolk, beaten

175 g (6 oz) plain flour

25 g (1 oz) cornflour

For the filling

2 tsp coffee granules

1 tsp warm water

4 chocolate-coated
fingers of fudge

2½ tbsp double cream

Custard Creams

INGREDIENTS

Makes 32

125 g (4 oz) butter

125 g (4 oz) caster sugar

1 egg yolk, beaten

200 g (7 oz) plain flour

40 g (1½ oz) custard powder or cornflour

1 tbsp milk

1 tbsp custard powder or cornflour

75 ml (3 fl oz) milk

50 g (2 oz) butter

40 g (1½ oz) icing sugar

1 egg yolk, beaten

1 tbsp single cream

1   Preheat the oven to 180°C (350°F/Gas 4). Lightly grease several baking sheets.

2   Put the butter and sugar in a bowl and beat until light and creamy. Beat in the egg yolk.

3   Sift together the flour and custard powder or cornflour. Add to the mixture and mix in thoroughly with the milk to make a smooth dough. Knead gently.

4   Roll out the dough on a floured surface to a 30 cm (12 in) square.

5   Cut into 4 cm (1½ in) squares using a pastry wheel or knife and place on the baking sheets.

6   Bake for 6-7 minutes until very lightly browned, then transfer to wire racks to cool.

7   Meanwhile, make the filling. Put the custard powder or cornflour in a small saucepan. Blend in the milk until smooth. Add the butter and icing sugar and bring to the boil, stirring constantly until thick.

8   Beat in the egg yolk and cream, cover and leave until cold.

9   Sandwich the biscuits together and keep in a cool place.

Strawberry Cheesecakes

1   Preheat the oven to 180°C (350°F/Gas 4). Lightly grease 2 or 3 baking sheets.

2   Put the butter and sugar in a bowl and beat until light and creamy. Beat in the egg yolk.

3   Mix together the flours, then add to the bowl. Mix in thoroughly to make a smooth dough. Knead gently.

4   Roll out the dough on a floured surface to 3 mm (⅛ in) thick. Cut out rounds with a 5.5 cm (2¼ in) fluted cutter. Place on baking sheets and remove centres from half of the rounds with a petits fours cutter. Knead and re-roll trimmings to cut out more rounds and tops until all the dough is used up.

5   Bake for 7-8 minutes until lightly browned. Transfer to wire racks to cool.

6   To make the filling, mix together cheese and cream. Spread a layer of cheese mixture and a layer of jam on the biscuit rounds and top with rings. Keep in a cool place.

COOK'S TIP
The cheese filling softens these biscuits quite quickly. To keep them crisp do not fill more than 3 hours before serving.

INGREDIENTS

Makes 20

125 g (4 oz) butter

75 g (3 oz) caster sugar

1 egg yolk, beaten

75 g (3 oz) self-raising flour

75 g (2 oz) plain wholemeal flour

150 g (5 oz) full-fat soft cheese

1½ tbsp single cream

150 g (5 oz) strawberry jam

Honey Brandy Snaps

INGREDIENTS

Makes 28

75 g (3 oz) butter

75 g (3 oz) soft light
brown sugar

75 g (3 oz) golden syrup

75 g (3 oz) plain flour

1 tsp ground ginger

finely grated zest of ½
lemon

1 tbsp brandy

300 ml (½ pint) whipping
cream

2 tbsp clear honey

finely grated rind of ½
lemon

2 tsp lemon juice

1   Preheat the oven to 190°C (375°F/Gas 5). Line several baking sheets with non-stick paper.

2   Put the butter, sugar and syrup into a saucepan and stir over a gentle heat until melted. Cool slightly.

3   Sift together the flour and ginger. Stir into the melted ingredients with the lemon rind and brandy.

4   Drop teaspoonfuls of the mixture onto the baking sheets, spacing them well apart, then flatten slightly. Bake for 7-8 minutes until lightly browned.

5   Leave the brandy snaps to cool for a few seconds before rolling them around wooden spoon handles or pencils. Place on wire racks to cool completely.

6   To make the filling, whip the cream until standing in soft peaks. Add the honey, lemon rind and juice and whip until thick.

7   Spoon the cream into a piping bag fitted with a small star nozzle and pipe into the brandy snaps.

COOK'S TIP
Cook these in batches of 4 or 5 at a time as they must be shaped while hot. If they harden before shaping, re-heat for a few seconds. To keep them crisp do not fill more than an hour before serving.

Tia Maria Tuiles

1   Preheat the oven to 180°C (350°F/Gas 4). Line several baking sheets with non-stick paper.

2   Put the egg whites in a clean, grease-free bowl. Whisk until just stiff, then gradually whisk in the sugar.

3   Fold in the butter and flour. Dissolve the coffee granules in Tia Maria and stir gently into the mixture.

4   Drop teaspoonfuls of the mixture onto the baking sheets, spacing them well apart. Spread into 5 cm (2 in) rounds. Bake for 7-8 minutes until lightly browned around the edges.

5   Remove biscuits from the baking sheets immediately and curve gently over rolling pins to shape.

6   Leave to cool slightly before transferring to wire racks to cool. Dredge with icing sugar.

COOK'S TIP
Tuiles are crisp, thin biscuits named after curved tiles whose shape they resemble. Cook in batches of only 6 or 7 at a time as they must be shaped while hot. If the biscuits harden before shaping, return them to the oven for a few seconds to soften slightly.

INGREDIENTS

Makes 40

3 egg whites

100 g (3½ oz) caster sugar

75 g (3 oz) unsalted butter, melted

65 g (2½ oz) plain flour, sifted

¾ tsp instant coffee granules

4 tsp Tia Maria

icing sugar to dredge

Muesli Cookies

INGREDIENTS

Makes 24

125 g (4 oz) butter

75 g (3 oz) light
muscovado sugar

1 egg, beaten

75 g (3 oz) plain flour

125 g (4 oz) muesli

50 g (2 oz) ground
almonds

1   Preheat the oven to 190°C (375°F/Gas 5). Lightly grease 2 or 3 baking sheets.

2   Put the butter and sugar in a bowl and beat until light and creamy. Beat in the egg.

3   Sift the flour into the bowl, then add the muesli and ground almonds and mix thoroughly.

4   Drop heaped teaspoonfuls of mixture onto the baking sheets, spacing them well apart. Flatten slightly.

5   Bake for about 10 minutes or until lightly browned. Transfer to a wire rack to cool.

COOK'S TIP
Use a Swiss-style muesli for best results. If you prefer a deluxe muesli chop the larger pieces of fruit and nut finely.

Linz Lattice

1   Lightly grease a shallow 28 x 18 cm (11 x 7 in) tin.

2   Put the butter and sugar in a bowl and beat until light and creamy. Gradually beat in the egg and almond essence.

3   Sift together the flours and spice. Work into the creamed mixture with the ground almonds to make a dough. Knead lightly.

4   Cut off two-thirds of the dough and roll out on a lightly floured surface to fit into the prepared tin. Press in well and spread the jam over the dough.

5   Roll out the remaining piece of dough to 4 mm (⅙ in) thick. Cut into 1 cm (½ in) strips. Arrange the strips in a lattice pattern over the jam. Chill for 30 minutes.

6   Preheat the oven to 180°C (350°F/Gas 4).

7   Brush the lattice with milk and bake for 20 minutes or until lightly browned.

8   Cool slightly in the tin. Cut into 3 pieces lengthwise and 5 widthwise to make 15 squares. Leave to cool completely, then dredge with icing sugar.

INGREDIENTS

Makes 15

125 g (4 oz) butter

75 g (3 oz) icing sugar, sifted

1 egg, beaten

few drops of almond essence

125 g (4 oz) plain flour

50 g (2 oz) self-raising flour

¾ tsp mixed spice

75 g (3 oz) ground almonds

2½ tbsp raspberry jam

milk to glaze

icing sugar to dredge

Hazelnut Florentines

INGREDIENTS

Makes 16

50 g (2 oz) butter

50 g (2 oz) caster sugar

2 tbsp golden syrup

40 g (1½ oz) plain flour

75 g (3 oz) roasted
hazelnuts, chopped

50 g (2 oz) glacé
cherries, chopped

50 g (2 oz) sultanas

25 g (1 oz) cut mixed
peel

finely grated rind of ½
lemon

50 g (2 oz) each of plain,
milk and white chocolate

1　Preheat the oven to 180°C (350°F/Gas 4). Line several baking sheets with non-stick paper.

2　Put the butter, sugar and syrup into a saucepan and stir over a gentle heat until melted. Cool slightly. Stir the flour into the melted mixture with the nuts, fruit and lemon rind.

3　Drop 16 heaped teaspoons of the mixture onto the baking sheets, spacing well apart. Shape into neat rounds. Bake for 10-11 minutes until lightly browned, then leave for a few minutes before transferring to a wire rack to cool.

4　To finish the Florentines melt each type of chocolate in small bowls placed over a pan of hot water. Spread the chocolate over the smooth side of each Florentine. Mark into wavy lines with a fork. Leave in a cool place to set.

COOK'S TIP
Use a good-quality chocolate for the best finish and melt it carefully. The bowl should fit the top of the pan exactly and should not touch the water beneath it. Use hot, not boiling water.

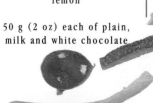

Sugar Pretzels

1 Lightly grease several baking sheets.

2 Put the butter and sugar in a bowl and beat until light and creamy. Beat in the egg, syrup and vanilla essence.

3 Sift flour into bowl and mix in to make a smooth dough. Knead lightly. Divide the dough into 40 pieces on a floured surface. Roll each piece into a thin strand about 25 cm (10 in) long.

4 To shape pretzels tie each strand in a loose knot and press the ends near to the top of each circle. Place on the baking sheets and chill for 30 minutes.

5 Preheat the oven to 190°C (375°F/Gas 5). Bake the pretzels for 9-10 minutes until very lightly browned. Transfer to wire racks to cool.

6 When cold, brush the pretzels with egg white and sprinkle with demerara sugar.

7 Place under a hot grill for about 1 minute until the sugar is just starting to bubble and brown. Return to wire racks to cool.

INGREDIENTS

Makes 40

125 g (4 oz) butter

125 g (4 oz) icing sugar, sifted

1 egg, beaten

1 tbsp golden syrup

few drops vanilla essence

250 g (9 oz) plain flour

To finish

1 egg white, beaten

65 g (2½ oz) demerara sugar

Caribbean Whirls

INGREDIENTS

Makes 30

125 g (4 oz) butter

75 g (3 oz) caster sugar

1 egg yolk

200 g (7 oz) plain flour

50 g (2 oz) creamed
coconut, coarsely grated

For the buttercream

125 g (4 oz) icing sugar,
sifted

50 g (2 oz) butter

2 tbsp whipping cream

2-3 tsp dark rum

extra raisins and finely
grated orange and lime
rinds to decorate

1   Preheat the oven to 180°C (350°F/Gas 4). Lightly grease 2 or 3 baking sheets.

2   Put the butter and sugar in a bowl and beat until light and creamy. Beat in the egg yolk.

3   Sift the flour into the bowl and add the coconut. Mix to make a soft dough and knead gently. Divide into 30 pieces and roll each piece into a ball. Place on the baking sheets and flatten slightly.

4   Bake for 16-18 minutes until lightly browned, then transfer to wire racks to cool.

5   Meanwhile, make the buttercream. Put the icing sugar, butter and cream in a bowl and beat until light and creamy. Add rum to taste. Spoon into a piping bag fitted with a small star nozzle.

6   Pipe whirls of buttercream on to the biscuits and decorate with raisins and orange and lime rinds. Keep in a cool place.

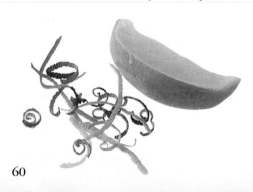

Chocolate Chip Crescents

1   Lightly grease 2 baking sheets.

2   Put the butter and sugar in a bowl and beat until light and creamy. Sift the flours into the mixture and work in by hand to make a soft dough. Gently knead in the chocolate chips.

3   Roll out on a floured surface to 8 mm (⅓ in) thick. Cut out crescents with a 6 cm (2½ in) cutter and place on the baking sheets. Knead and re-roll trimmings to cut out more crescents until the dough is used up. Chill for 30 minutes.

4   Preheat oven to 160°C (325°F/Gas 3). Bake the biscuits for 20-25 minutes until very lightly browned. Transfer to a wire rack to cool.

5   Melt the chocolate in a small bowl placed over a pan of hot water. Coat half of each crescent with melted chocolate and place on a sheet of foil or non-stick paper. Leave in a cool place to set.

INGREDIENTS

Makes 24

125 g (4oz) butter

40 g (1½oz) caster sugar

140 g (4½oz) plain flour

25 g (1 oz) rice flour

40 g (1½oz) plain chocolate chips

125 g (4 oz) plain chocolate to finish

Apple Crumbles

INGREDIENTS

Makes 16

225 g (8 oz) plain flour

125 g (4 oz) butter,
chilled and diced

25 g (1 oz) demerara
sugar

2 egg yolks

For the topping

125 g (4 oz) plain flour

1 tsp ground cinnamon

50 g (2 oz) butter,
chilled and diced

1 large dessert apple

2 tsp lemon juice

50 g (2 oz) demerara
sugar

1   Preheat the oven to 160°C (325°F/Gas 3). Lightly grease 2 18 cm (7 in) sandwich tins.

2   To make the base, sift the flour into a bowl. Rub in the butter until the mixture resembles fine breadcrumbs. Stir in the sugar. Add the egg yolks and mix to make a firm dough. Knead gently.

3   Divide the dough into 2 pieces. Roll out each piece on a lightly floured surface to fit the sandwich tins. Press in well. Bake for 20 minutes.

4   Meanwhile, prepare the topping. Sift the flour and cinnamon into a bowl. Rub in the butter until the mixture resembles fine breadcrumbs.

5   Finely grate the apple and toss in lemon juice. Stir into the rubbed-in mixture with the sugar.

6   Spoon the topping over the bases and return to the oven for about 35 minutes until browned. Mark each round into 8 pieces and cool in the tins.

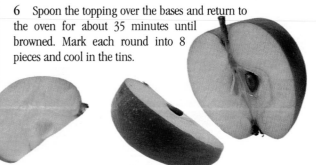

Viennese Pinks

1   Preheat the oven to 180°C (350°F/Gas 4). Lightly grease several baking sheets.

2   Put the butter and sugar in a bowl and beat until light and creamy. Sift the flour and blancmange powder into the mixture and work in well.

3   Spoon the mixture into a piping bag fitted with a medium star nozzle. Pipe 7.5 cm (3 in) lengths onto the baking sheets.

4   Bake for about 20 minutes until very lightly browned. Leave for a few minutes before transferring to a wire rack to cool.

5   Melt the chocolate in a small bowl placed over a pan of hot water. Dip the ends of each biscuit in chocolate and place on a sheet of foil or non-stick paper. Leave in a cool place to set.

COOK'S TIPS
Vary the flavour by using different blancmange powders. If the mixture is rather stiff to pipe, soften with a few drops of milk.

INGREDIENTS

Makes 24

225 g (8 oz) butter

50 g (2 oz) icing sugar, sifted

200 g (7oz) plain flour

75 g (3 oz) strawberry-flavour blancmange powder

125 g (4 oz) white chocolate to decorate

Choc and Oat Surprises

INGREDIENTS

Makes 20

125 g (4 oz) butter

75 g (3 oz) caster sugar

75 g (3 oz) self-raising
flour

1 tbsp cocoa

50 g (2 oz) rolled oats

75 g (3 oz) marzipan

2 tbsp rolled oats for
coating

25 g (1oz) plain
chocolate drops

1   Preheat the oven to 190°C (375°F/Gas 5). Lightly grease 2 baking sheets.

2   Put the butter and sugar in a bowl and beat until light and creamy. Sift together the flour and cocoa. Add to the bowl with the rolled oats and work in to make a fairly firm dough.

3   Divide both the dough and the marzipan into 20 pieces. Roll the marzipan pieces into balls and wrap a piece of dough around each one, pressing it gently over the marzipan.

4   Roll each ball in oats to coat and place on the baking sheets. Top with chocolate drops.

5   Bake for about 10 minutes, or until just firm to touch. Transfer to a wire rack to cool.

Triple Chocolate Shortcakes

1   Put the butter and sugar in a bowl and beat until light and creamy. Sift the flour, cornflour and cocoa into the mixture and work in well to make a smooth dough. Knead lightly.

2   Roll out the dough on a floured surface to fit a 28 x 18 cm (11 x 7 in) Swiss roll tin. Press in lightly and chill for 30 minutes.

3   Preheat the oven to 160°C (325°F/Gas 3). Bake the shortcake for about 25 minutes or until just firm to touch.

4   Leave to cool for a few minutes, then mark into squares, cutting into 4 lengthwise and 6 widthwise. Cut each square into 2 triangles and leave to cool in the tin.

5   To finish, melt the plain chocolate in a small bowl over a pan of hot water. Dip the shortcakes in the chocolate to coat evenly. Place on a sheet of foil or non-stick paper and leave in a cool place to set.

6   Melt the white chocolate in the same way and pipe or drizzle over the shortcake triangles. Leave in a cool place to set.

INGREDIENTS

Makes 48

225 g (8 oz) butter

125 g (4 oz) icing sugar, sifted

200 g (7 oz) plain flour

50 g (2 oz) cornflour

2 tbsp cocoa

To finish

450 g (1 lb) plain chocolate, chopped

75 g (3 oz) white chocolate

Almond Hearts

INGREDIENTS

Makes 80

200 g (7 oz) ground
almonds

75 g (3 oz) caster sugar

50 g (2 oz) icing sugar,
sifted

1 egg, beaten

2 tsp brandy

extra beaten egg to glaze

25 g (1 oz) flaked
almonds

1   Preheat the oven to 180°C (350°F/Gas 4). Line 2 or 3 baking sheets with non-stick paper.

2   Put the ground almonds, caster sugar and icing sugar into a bowl. Mix together. Stir in the egg and brandy to make a firm dough. Knead very lightly.

3   Roll out the dough on a lightly floured surface to 6 mm (¼ in) thick. Brush with egg to glaze and sprinkle with flaked almonds.

4   Cut out shapes with a small heart-shaped cutter and place on the baking sheets. Push trimmings together to keep flaked almonds on top and cut out more hearts until all the dough is used up.

5   Bake for 10-12 minutes until lightly browned, then transfer to wire racks to cool.

Mother's Day Flowers

1 Preheat the oven to 180°C (350°F/Gas 4). Lightly grease 2 baking sheets.

2 Put the butter and sugar in a bowl and beat until light and creamy. Beat in the egg yolks.

3 Sift flour into the mixture, add the cream and work in well.

4 Spoon the mixture into a piping bag fitted with a medium star nozzle. Pipe 12 flower shapes on to the baking sheets.

5 Bake for 12-14 minutes until lightly browned. Leave to stand for a few minutes, then transfer to a wire rack to cool.

6 Meanwhile, make the icing. Blend the icing sugar with the rose or orange flower water until smooth and fairly thick. Use to ice biscuits, creating a neat and even surface.

7 Decorate with crystallized flower pieces and orange rind and leave to dry.

INGREDIENTS

Makes 12

50 g (2 oz) butter

40 g (1½ oz) caster sugar

2 egg yolks, beaten

125 g (4 oz) self-raising flour

4 tsp single cream

To decorate

50 g (2 oz) icing sugar, sifted

1½ -2 tsp rose water or orange flower water

crystallized flower pieces and finely grated orange rind

Easter Biscuits

INGREDIENTS

Makes 10

125 g (4 oz) butter

75 g (3 oz) caster sugar

1 egg, beaten

225 g (8 oz) plain flour

½ tsp mixed spice

½ tsp ground cinnamon

50 g (2 oz) currants
50 g (2 oz) cut mixed
peel

caster sugar to dredge

1 Preheat the oven to 190°C (375°F/Gas 5). Lightly grease several baking sheets.

2 Put the butter and sugar in a bowl and beat until light and creamy. Gradually beat in the egg.

3 Sift the flour and spice into a bowl. Add the currants and peel, then mix to make a firm dough and knead lightly.

4 Roll out the dough on a lightly floured surface to 6 mm (¼ in) thick. Cut out rounds with a 10 cm (4 in) fluted cutter and place on the baking sheets. Knead and re-roll trimmings to cut out more rounds until all the dough is used up.

5 Bake for 15 minutes until or lightly browned. Dredge with caster sugar and transfer to a wire rack to cool.

Mocha Meringue Eggs

1   Preheat the oven to 140°C (275°F/Gas 1). Line 2 baking sheets with non-stick paper.

2   Put the egg white in a clean, grease-free bowl. Whisk until stiff but not dry. Gradually whisk in half of the sugar. Fold in the remainder with the chocolate and cornflour.

3   Drop rounded dessertspoons of the mixture on to the baking sheets and smooth into half egg shapes. Bake for 50-55 minutes until firm to the touch. Cool on the baking sheets.

4   Meanwhile make the filling. Put the coffee and water in a small bowl and stir to dissolve. Melt the chocolate in a bowl placed over a pan of hot water. Whip half the cream until standing in soft peaks. Whisk the remainder into the melted chocolate with the coffee until thick. Fold in the remaining whipped cream.

5   Spoon the chocolate cream into a piping bag fitted with a small star nozzle. Pipe some cream on to the flat sides of the meringue eggs to sandwich together, decorate with the remainder.

6   Tie ribbons around the eggs to finish. Keep chilled.

INGREDIENTS

Makes 8

2 egg whites

175 g (6 oz) caster sugar

125 g (4 oz) plain chocolate, grated

50 g (2 oz) cornflour, sifted

coloured ribbons to decorate

4 tsp instant coffee granules

2 tsp warm water

125 g (4 oz) plain chocolate

150 ml (5 fl oz) whipping cream

Halloween Faces

INGREDIENTS

Makes 12

125 g (4 oz) butter

50 g (2 oz) caster sugar

150 g (5 oz) plain flour

2 tsp cocoa, sifted

1 Preheat the oven to 190°C (375°F/Gas 5). Lightly grease 2 or 3 baking sheets.

2 Put the butter and sugar in a bowl and beat until light and creamy. Sift in the flour and work in to make a soft dough. Knead.

3 Divide the dough in half on a floured surface. Knead the cocoa into one half.

4 Roll out each mixture to 8 mm (⅓ in) thick. Using a sharp knife cut out 7.5 cm (3 in) faces and place on baking sheets. Cut out eye triangles and mouths from the trimmings and press gently onto the faces. Knead and re-roll the trimmings to cut out more faces until all the dough is used up.

5 Bake for about 8 minutes or until just firm to the touch. Stand for a few minutes before transferring to a wire rack to cool.

Christmas Trees

1   Lightly grease 2 or 3 baking sheets.

2   Put the butter and sugar in a bowl and beat until light and creamy. Mix together the flours, then add to the mixture and work in to make a soft dough. Knead gently.

3   Roll out the dough on a floured surface to 4 mm (⅙ in) thick. Cut out trees about 8 cm (3½ in) tall and place on the baking sheets. Knead and re-roll the trimmings to cut out more trees until all the dough is used up. Chill for 30 minutes.

4   Preheat the oven to 180°C (350°F/Gas 4). Bake the biscuits for about 12 minutes until very lightly browned.

5   Transfer to a wire rack to cool, then decorate with icing sugar.

COOK'S TIP
Use templates made from thin card to mask centres or edges of Christmas trees, then dredge with icing sugar to decorate.

INGREDIENTS

Makes 24

125 g (4 oz) butter

40 g (1½ oz) soft light brown sugar

65 g (2½ oz) plain wholemeal flour

50 g (2 oz) plain flour, sifted

25 g (1 oz) rice flour, sifted

icing sugar to decorate

Scandinavian Spiced Biscuits

INGREDIENTS

Makes 18

50 g (2 oz) butter

50 g (2 oz) golden syrup

40 g (1½ oz) demerara
sugar

140 g (4½ oz) plain flour

¾ tsp mixed spice

½ tsp bicarbonate of soda

½ egg yolk

finely grated zest of ½
lemon

about ½ an egg white

75-125 g (3-4 oz) icing
sugar, sifted

food colourings, coloured
dragées

1   Preheat the oven to 180°C (350°F/Gas 4). Lightly grease 2 baking sheets.

2   Put the butter, syrup and sugar into a saucepan and stir over a gentle heat until melted. Cool slightly.

3   Sift together the flour, spice and bicarbonate of soda. Mix into the melted ingredients with the egg yolk and lemon rind.

4   Turn out the dough on to a floured surface and knead lightly. Roll out to 6 mm (¼ in) thick and cut out shapes about 6 cm (2½ in) in size using tree cutters. Place on the baking sheets. Using a skewer, make a small hole near the top of each biscuit. Knead and re-roll trimmings to cut out more shapes.

5   Bake for 12-14 minutes until lightly browned. Push a skewer through each hole again to ensure they are large enough to thread ribbons through. Transfer to a wire rack to cool.

6   Meanwhile, make the icing. Beat the egg white until frothy. Gradually beat in the sugar until the icing is smooth and thick.

7   Colour the icing if wished and spread or pipe onto the biscuits. Decorate with dragées and leave to dry.

8   Thread the biscuits with ribbons to hang on the Christmas tree or pack to give as gifts.

Chocolate Crackers

1   Preheat the oven to 180°C (350°F/Gas 4). Line several baking sheets with non-stick paper.

2   Put the egg whites in a clean, grease-free bowl. Whisk until just stiff, then gradually whisk in the sugar. Fold in the butter and flour.

3   Drop small dessertspoons of the mixture onto the baking sheets, spacing them well apart. Spread into 10 cm (4 in) rounds. Bake for 7-8 minutes until lightly browned around the edges.

4   Immediately remove the biscuits from the baking sheets and roll around pencils to shape. Place on a wire rack to cool.

5   Meanwhile, make the filling. Melt the chocolate and butter with brandy to taste in a small bowl over a pan of hot water. Remove from the heat and stir in icing sugar and cream. Leave to cool, then chill until thick enough to pipe.

6   Spoon the filling into a piping bag fitted with a 6mm (¼ in) plain nozzle. Pipe into the centres of the rolled biscuits. Wrap the biscuits in coloured foil to make crackers.

COOK'S TIP
Cook these in batches of 4-5 as they have to be handled while still hot. Keep filled and wrapped crackers in an airtight container in the refrigerator for 3-4 days.

INGREDIENTS

Makes 20

3 egg whites

100 g (3½ oz) caster sugar

75 g (3 oz) unsalted butter, melted

65 g (2½ oz) plain flour, sifted

50 g (2 oz) plain chocolate

15 g (½ oz) butter

1-2 tsp brandy

2 tbsp single cream

25 g (1 oz) icing sugar, sifted

Amaretti

INGREDIENTS

Makes 30

1 egg white

1½ tsp Amaretto liqueur

200 g (7 oz) icing sugar

130 g (4¼ oz) sweet almonds, blanched and finely ground

20 g (¾ oz) bitter almonds, blanched and finely ground

finely grated rind of ½ lemon

icing sugar to dredge

coloured tissue paper if wrapping

1   Preheat the oven to 180°C (350°F/Gas 4). Line 2 or 3 baking sheets with non-stick paper.

2   Beat together the egg white and Amaretto.

3   Sift the icing sugar into a bowl. Add all the ground almonds and the lemon rind. Make a well in the centre. Pour in the egg white and mix to make a paste.

4   Divide the paste into 30 pieces and roll each piece into a ball. Place on the baking sheets. Bake for 12-15 minutes until lightly browned.

5   Dredge with icing sugar and transfer to wire racks to cool. Wrap in tissue paper to pack if giving as gifts.

COOK'S TIP
If you cannot get bitter almonds use all sweet ones. In this recipe grind the almonds yourself for the best flavour.

Snowballs

1   Put the chocolate, butter and brandy in a heatproof bowl. Place over a pan of hot water, stirring occasionally, until melted.

2   Stir the biscuit crumbs, coconut, apricots and cherries into the melted mixture. Leave until slightly firm.

3   Roll the mixture into 18 balls about the size of walnuts, then roll in extra coconut to coat.

4   Refrigerate for about 2 hours until firmly set.

INGREDIENTS

Makes 18

225 g (8 oz) white chocolate, chopped

50 g (2 oz) butter

4 tsp brandy

65 g (2½ oz) plain biscuit crumbs

40 g (1½ oz) desiccated coconut

25 g (1 oz) ready-to-eat dried apricots, finely chopped

25 g (1 oz) glacé cherries, finely chopped

an extra 40 g (1½ oz) desiccated coconut for rolling

Toffee Fingers

INGREDIENTS

Makes 12

125 g (4 oz) golden syrup

65 g (2½ oz) soft light brown sugar

40 g (1½ oz) butter

50 g (2 oz) rice breakfast cereal

For the filling

175 g (6 oz) cream toffees

50 g (2 oz) butter

50 ml (2 fl oz) single cream

For the topping

75 g (3 oz) milk chocolate

25 g (1 oz) butter

1   Lightly grease a shallow 18 cm (7 in) square tin. Line the base with non-stick paper.

2   To make the base put the syrup, sugar and butter into a saucepan. Stir over a gentle heat until melted. Bring to the boil. Stir the cereal into the mixture, then press into the prepared tin.

3   To make the filling put the toffees, butter and cream into a saucepan. Stir over a gentle heat until melted. Bring to the boil. Pour the filling over the base. Refrigerate for about 1 hour until firmly set.

4   To make the topping put the chocolate and butter into a heat-proof bowl. Place over a pan of hot water, stirring occasionally, until melted.

5   Spread the topping over the toffee filling and refrigerate for about 1 hour until set.

6   Carefully remove the slab from the tin and peel off the paper. Cut the square in half and cut each half into 6 fingers. Keep refrigerated until serving.

Tropical Treats

1 Lightly grease a shallow 20 cm (8 in) square tin. Line the base with non-stick paper.

2 Put the butter, syrup, cocoa and coffee into a saucepan and stir over a gentle heat until melted.

3 Stir the cereal, banana chips, coconut and raisins into the melted mixture. Turn into the prepared tin and press down well. Refrigerate for 2-3 hours until firmly set.

4 Carefully remove the slab from the tin and peel off the paper. Cut into 3 each way to make squares. Cut each square into 2 triangles to serve.

COOK'S TIP
Keep no-bake biscuits in a container in the refrigerator for up to 10 days.

INGREDIENTS

Makes 18

125 g (4 oz) butter

4 tbsp golden syrup

1 ½ tbsp cocoa

2 tsp instant coffee granules

175 g (6 oz) crunchy oat cereal, crushed

50 g (2 oz) banana chips, chopped

50 g (2 oz) desiccated coconut

50 g (2 oz) raisins, chopped

Date and Walnut Slices

INGREDIENTS

Makes 20

125 g (4 oz) butter

25 g (1 oz) demerara
sugar

3 tbsp golden syrup

finely grated rind of ½
lemon

175 g (6 oz) wholewheat
cereal flakes, lightly
crushed

150 g (5 oz) stoned
dates, finely chopped

75 g (3 oz) walnuts,
finely chopped

1   Lightly grease a shallow 20 cm (8 in) square tin. Line the base with non-stick paper.

2   Put the butter, sugar, syrup and lemon rind into a saucepan. Stir over a gentle heat until melted.

3   Stir the cereal, dates and walnuts into the melted mixture. Turn into the prepared tin and press down well. Refrigerate for 2-3 hours until firmly set.

4   Carefully remove the slab from the tin and peel off the paper. Cut into 4 slices, then cut each slice into 5 pieces. Keep refrigerated until serving.

Orange Muesli Bars

1   Lightly grease a shallow 20 cm (8 in) square tin. Line the base with non-stick paper.

2   Break the chocolate into pieces. Put it into a saucepan with the butter, honey and orange rind and juice. Stir over a gentle heat until melted.

3   Stir the muesli into melted mixture. Turn into the prepared tin and press down well. Refrigerate for 2-3 hours until firmly set.

4   Carefully remove the slab from the tin and peel off the paper. Cut the square in half and cut each half into 8 bars to serve.

COOK'S TIP
In this recipe chocolate can safely be melted directly over heat in the saucepan. The addition of a large quantity of other ingredients prevents it from scorching.

INGREDIENTS

Makes 16

225 g (8 oz) plain
chocolate

125 g (4 oz) butter

4 tbsp honey

finely grated rind of 2
oranges

4 tbsp orange juice

450 g (1 lb) Swiss-style
muesli

Index

PRINTED IN BELGIUM BY
proost
INTERNATIONAL BOOK PRODUCTION